This book will take you on a journey to freedom in easy and playful ways, guiding you to release your past and create the future you truly want and deserve.

THE ART of TAPPING

A Combination of Emotional Freedom Technique and Expressive Art Therapy

MONIKA MARGUERITE LUX

BALBOA
PRESS
A DIVISION OF HAY HOUSE

Balboa Press books may be ordered through booksellers or by contacting:

Balboa Press
A Division of Hay House
1663 Liberty Drive
Bloomington, IN 47403
www.balboapress.com
1 (877) 407-4847

Because of the dynamic nature of the Internet, any web addresses or links contained in this book may have changed since publication and may no longer be valid. The views expressed in this work are solely those of the author and do not necessarily reflect the views of the publisher, and the publisher hereby disclaims any responsibility for them.

The author of this book does not dispense medical advice or prescribe the use of any technique as a form of treatment for physical, emotional, or medical problems without the advice of a physician, either directly or indirectly. The intent of the author is only to offer information of a general nature to help you in your quest for emotional and spiritual well-being. In the event you use any of the information in this book for yourself, which is your constitutional right, the author and the publisher assume no responsibility for your actions.

Any people depicted in stock imagery provided by Thinkstock are models, and such images are being used for illustrative purposes only. Certain stock imagery © Thinkstock.

Print information available on the last page.

ISBN: 978-1-5043-8095-9 (sc)
ISBN: 978-1-5043-8129-1 (e)

Balboa Press rev. date: 05/24/2017

ABOUT THE BOOK

Tapping meets Art Therapy

Discover a gentle emotional release technique that is part of "The BalanCHIng® Method", a unique, therapeutic system of healing that has liberated innumerable people from their emotional burden, opening the doors to greater levels of wealth, freedom, health, joy and fulfilling relationships by simply accessing and releasing what is buried deep within. This transformational method, developed by Monika Marguerite Lux, will take you on a journey to freedom in easy and playful ways, guiding you to release your past and create the future you truly want and deserve.

For more information visit:

- **www.balanching.wordpress.com**
- **www.facebook.com/balanching**

Contact me:

- **balanching@hotmail.com**

Skype, What's App and Facebook Video Call Sessions available!

Welcome to The Art Of Tapping!

With this book, you can take back control of your life!

Oscar Wilde once said "I don't want to be at the mercy of my emotions. I want to use them, to enjoy them, and to dominate them." Remember, you are not your emotions!

All the effort you put into releasing trapped emotions will give you a sunnier outlook on life and teach you that you have a choice to feel good or not.

Healing also means re-claiming your childhood innocence with all the miracles around you and remembering WHO you really are! This book invites you to paint, to draw and to play. It also invites you to tap on everything that comes to mind during the drawing process, even if it might sound, look or feel a bit crazy to you. Try to look at everything through the eyes of a child.

Have the courage to acknowledge your trauma, show compassion and forgiveness for yourself, release your past and move on stronger than ever!

DISCLAIMER AND NOTE TO READERS

The information provided within this book is for general informational purposes only. While the author tries to keep the information up-to-date and correct, there are no representations or warranties, express or implied, about the completeness, accuracy, reliability, suitability or availability with respect to the information, products, services, or related graphics contained in this book for any purpose. Any use of this information is at your own risk. The material in this book is for informational purposes only. As each individual situation is unique you should use proper discretion, in consultation with a healthcare practitioner, before undertaking the exercises and techniques described in this book.

The author expressly disclaims responsibility for any adverse effects that may result from the use or application of the book. Direction given in the book is merely a guideline for its use.

The content of this book is not intended to be a substitute for professional medical advice, diagnosis, or treatment. Always seek the advice of your physician or other qualified health provider with any questions you may have regarding a medical condition. Never disregard professional medical advice or delay in seeking it because of something you have read in this book.

The methods describe within this eBook are the author's personal thoughts. They are not intended to be a definitive set of instructions for this project. You may discover there are other methods and materials to accomplish the same end result.

TABLE OF CONTENTS

PREFACE

You may ask me how the "Art Of Tapping" was born.

It all started when I was working with a teenager suffering from high levels of anxiety and panic attacks.

When I looked at her sitting across the table from me, I suddenly remembered my first encounter with art therapy and how deeply it had touched me as a client. Intuitively I felt that this was the one and only way to be able to build rapport and establish a safe place quickly.

I asked my client if she could draw on a piece of paper what happened when she was in a situation that induced a panic attack. She drew a picture with numerous shapes in different colours. Her hands were sweating and I immediately started the tapping process. "Even though I'm surrounded by so many different shapes and it feels overwhelming and scary at times, I deeply and completely love, accept and forgive myself." We tapped on many aspects like "shapes moving around, while I am paralyzed" and "I just don't know what to do… I'm so scared". After a couple of rounds, I saw the tension dissipate. My client opened her fists and her body started to loosen up more and more.

I asked her which of the shapes belonged to her and she told me that it was missing completely. We found out that her unique shape was the heart. "Wow," I said "that's the most important shape ever. Please add it to the other shapes." She drew a tiny heart because there was not much space left on the paper. I started tapping again "Even though I feel very small and unimportant, I deeply and completely love, accept and forgive myself." and "this tiny heart amidst all the big shapes… they are invading my space… they are intimidating… I don't feel safe…" etc.

"I would like to see a bigger heart." I encouraged her and she said "There's no space; it would overlap the others." "That's ok." I answered and smiled at her. Now, she drew her heart in the middle of the picture and indeed it was overlapping a few of the other shapes. We started tapping again: "Even though my shape is overlapping other shapes, I deeply and completely love, accept and forgive myself." "It is ok to overlap… it is ok to move as well… it is ok to interact… it can be fun to move and socialize with others… it might not be so difficult… it makes me curious to learn more about the others… what if it's exciting to mingle with different shapes…"etc.

We talked about how we can learn from others and how they can learn from us and a few sessions down the line she told me that her whole world and perspective had changed through exercises like that.

Now we were able to develop a mental, emotional and behavioural strategy for future scary moments and from there we went into preventing panic attacks from escalating and recognizing the triggers. Those steps helped building self-awareness and self-confidence. My client learned who she was and about her strengths and skill set. She discovered how fear and self-doubt robbed her of her full potential and how feeding the soul with self-compassion and self-forgiveness gave her wings to soar and set her free.

"As soon as you trust yourself, you will know how to live." — Johann Wolfgang von Goethe

"If you want to soar in life, you must first learn to F.L.Y (First Love Yourself)" – Mark Sterling

The transformational process was incredible and so I continued to focus on this new path that had opened before me. And finally, I decided that this technique had to be perpetuated in a book.

Testimonial:

After participating in conventional therapies, my teenage daughter who has crippling anxiety, was more anxious than ever and began having panic attacks while out in public spaces, she was not able to go out unsupervised. We decided that she needed to try something different and found that Monika offered dance therapy which she was very excited about. After a few visits of Monika's unconditional support, kindness, acceptance, and love she began to trust and has excelled far beyond what we thought possible. She is now able to go out socially and has decided to go into the public high school after being homeschooled for her whole life. Monika has helped to give her insight and control over her anxiety and we thank her for changing our daughters' life!

Catherine C. and John B., British Columbia

QUOTES ABOUT TAPPING

I've always admired Louise Hay and read all her books. "Du kannst es! Durch Gedankenkraft die Illusion der Begrenztheit überwinden" / "I can do it! How to Use Affirmations to Change Your Life" was my first book to buy while I have been studying Applied Kinesiology.

This is what Louise Hay says about EFT:

"Have you tried tapping yet? I've done a little bit of tapping in the past few months. I'm what you would call a "newbie" to the tapping world.

When I first heard about using tapping or EFT (Emotional Freedom Technique), I thought it was delightful that something this simple and easy could really work.

Tapping, just like affirmations, is another wonderful tool that can help us to let go of our limiting thoughts and negative programming from our past.

And I do love the way the tapping process first releases the negative programming and then the affirmations help create more positive change and health in our lives.

Let's affirm: *Today I give myself the gift of freedom from the past. I tap with joy into the now.*"

https://www.healyourlife.com/have-you-tried-tapping

And here is another quote by Jack Canfield, originator of the #1 New York Times best-selling "Chicken Soup For The Soul" series and "Tapping Into Ultimate Success":

"EFT is the most powerful new transformational technology to come along in years..."

https://www.healyourlife.com/tap-away-your-stress

EFT STORIES

My own story

I have been with EFT for 15 years. I started with Applied Kinesiology. First, I learned how to test 42 muscles in Touch For Health. Then it was about 14 muscles and I thought "yep, slowly we are going to approach a technique that resonants with me." I learned about Roger Callahan and finally I was taught EFT. I immediately fell in love with this fast and effective technique that could be taken everywhere and used anytime. Meanwhile it became second nature to me. When I wake up from a nightmare in the middle of the night I tap myself back to sleep in my mind. Yes, that's right, I don't do the physical tapping because I'm too tired. I can internally feel myself tapping on all the points when I do it mentally and focus on the intention of going back to sleep as fast as possible.

"Our intentions create our reality. Intentions directly affect our metabolism and consequently every aspect of our health. It is common knowledge in the scientific community that our intentions influence our healing processes." ~ Dr. Adam McLeod

Of course, I use EFT during the day as well. Actually, as soon as I get triggered and feel emotionally out of balance. It just happened a few days ago. I was on my way to work when my eyes caught a black plastic bag in the middle of the road. Tears were shooting into my eyes and my heart felt heavily filled with sadness. I didn't have to ask myself what was going on in this very moment. I just knew. About 12 years ago, I was on my way to work when I saw something black laying in the middle of the road. First I thought it could be dirt lost by a truck or a black garbage bag. As I came closer I had to discover that my black and white cat had been killed by a car. I was devastated. It had been the third cat that was ripped out of my life and my heart broke in pieces. As a therapist, focused on emotional release I had worked on and through those deaths multiple times and everything seemed dealt with. But with time and studying EFT in depth, I learned that an incident has many aspects.

Gary Craig refers to the term "aspects" as "parts" of an event. Within those events, aspects are the parts of the experience, and it's vital that we identify all the aspects of an event, and tap on each one till it loses its emotional charge.

Obviously, I had overseen an aspect of this past traumatic event and it had been triggered by the plastic bag. I immediately started to tap the side of my hand against the steering wheel, saying the affirmation and then tapping through the sequence. I had released the aspect before I arrived at work and felt balanced again.

Another incident happened some years ago in Manitoba, when I accompanied a farmer to an abandoned house in the prairies. We had to take a narrow steep gravel road towards the property and I felt panic coming up inside of me. My heart started to race and I grabbed whatever I could to hold on. Of course, I was unable to explain why I was so scared going down that hill. For the entire ride, I was wondering about my reaction and if it had to do with my fear of heights. At home, I tapped but nothing seemed to come up, which is very unusual for me. I decided to let go of the "why" and see what would happen.

After three days, it popped up very suddenly while I was sitting in my car again. I remembered that I had tried to please my father to get his attention and love since I was very little. I knew that he loved skiing, so I wanted to learn this activity in order to accompany him on his holidays. You have to know, he never took my mom and me with him. He was a very impatient man and didn't want to be bothered by children and their questions. He often yelled at me when I didn't understand at the first go. In this case, I had convinced him to teach me how to ski. He had shown me the snowplough technique in front of our home and the following weekend he took me to my first ski hill. I've never seen a ski lift but he took me between his legs and we managed to arrive at the top of the hill. Up there he reminded me of the technique and encouraged me to go downhill. I looked down and it seemed too steep for me. I started to shiver and cry. My father got very angry and yelled "Do you think we went all the way up here for nothing? Do you think I have nothing else to do? Do you think I want to waste my time with you?" and then he pushed me. Of course, I lost balance and fell and was more devastated than ever.

This had been the first and last time in terms of downhill skiing. I had never approached this sport again until I tried and enjoyed cross-country skiing after immigrating to Manitoba.

Anyways, I pulled my car to the side and tapped on the incident with all aspects that came to mind and indeed, the next time we drove to the farm, I was only left with my fear of heights which is pretty manageable.

You may ask why I don't tap on my fear of heights. I know that the subconscious mind protects us all the time. My fear of heights protected me from jumping from a bridge when I was suicidal around my twenties. I'm very grateful to be alive and I guess, I still want to keep my lifesaver, even though it's sometimes uncomfortable.

The Sore Shoulder

In one of my seminars I had a client with a sore shoulder. I explained to her that pain and disease are often caused by buried emotions and asked her when it started. She told me about a car accident almost 20 years ago and that she'd got away just with some bruises. The doctors always had reassured her that everything had been fine with her shoulder. I encouraged her to tell me about the accident and she first refused because it had happened so long ago and she had dealt with this incident already. But I could see how nervous she got and that her body started to tremble. I took her hand and just tapped on the Gamut point and the side of her hand while she tried hard to fight back the tears forming in her eyes.

We revealed many aspects together and with releasing each of them my client became calmer and at the end she was at peace. She was able to move her arm freely and without pain.

It showed again, that supressed emotions can be the root of disease, pain, depression and PTSD (Post Traumatic Stress Disorder), to just name some examples.

The main aspect we discovered was guilt. My client had convinced her best friend to join the "gang" on this trip and this friend was the most injured passenger. In fact, she became paralyzed through this accident. Can you imagine, how this burden may cause shoulder pain? Going through the trauma again was causing a lot of emotional pain and many tears were cried though the process. But in the end my client was free; free of guilt and free of pain.

Weight Loss

I once worked with a client who had tried to lose weight for almost ten years and it had been an up and down, a losing and regaining all the time. My client was very frustrated and at the end of her wits as she had tried everything, from consulting nutritionists, trying all kinds of diets to visiting various doctors without any results.

I am very intuitive and when I work with somebody I connect to the energy field very quickly. I sensed that this issue had its roots in her childhood. I decided to do a family constellation (Bert

Hellinger: Orders Of Love and Acknowledging What Is). Usually this is a group therapy but it's possible to do it one-on-one, using objects to represent the family members or the issues: e.g. figures or stuffed animals. So, I let her choose representatives for herself, her siblings and her parents and asked her to put them in the middle of the room without overthinking it.

I was surprised seeing her and her siblings standing in a row one behind the other, facing the father and I asked her what she thought about this picture. She got very emotional and told me that once a week the father used to spank all the children with a belt for disobedience. The youngest sister had been obese and was punished hardest.

"How many of your siblings are overweight right now?" I asked her immediately and she told me that all of them more or less had some weight issues.

I explained to her that there are unconscious family loyalties and that out of love and for the protection of the youngest sibling all the other siblings took on some weight. I invited my client into the constellation, to step into her place (her field) and tell her sister "I did it for you to protect you and to take away some of your pain that weighed you down. I was the older one, I was able to carry more weight than you. But now we are all adults and it's not necessary anymore. Now I finally can let go of the weight and so, I choose to let go."

Then, we started tapping on every aspect of the trauma, releasing the hidden and destructive family dynamics of her childhood. We tapped on forgiveness for self and others, and that every family member has his or her very own story.

I told my client that the parents of our generation still had to deal with war trauma and shared my own family history:

"All her life, my own mother had been depressed because she had been traumatized by the constant threat to her life through the air raids she had experienced as a child. And my grandmother had to flee from the Red Army with my father and his brother in a cold and overfilled train, relocating from Breslau (Wrocław, Poland) to Rosenheim (Germany). My grandfather had been missing in action and it took the White Cross ten years after the war to inform my grandmother about his death that had occurred in a Russian prison camp. She had been waiting for her husband for ten years because she didn't want to believe that he wasn't alive anymore, after all she had a letter where he had promised to come back."

Significant insight through the constellation, increased awareness of my client's emotions, thoughts and behaviors and EFT helped her heal herself emotionally and finally lose her first pounds.

The fairy and the bowl of porridge

In Germany, I have a very good friend who is a hairdresser and at that time worked out of her home. I came for my appointment and she told me that her youngest daughter had the flu. She asked me if I would excuse her when she had to look after her from time to time. Of course, I didn't mind as I loved this little red-haired girl very much. Soon she was sitting on my lap, not able to sleep any longer. I felt how feverish she was and started to give Reiki while I was holding her. My friend invited me to stay for lunch and had prepared a bowl of porridge for the little one. But of course, there is a lack of appetite that comes with those flues and I pondered how I could convince her to eat at least a little bit.

The girl gave me a clue. She was looking all around the room to find her fairy but couldn't see her. I told her that I could see fairies too and that I had discovered this magical being sitting on rim of the bowl. "Oh dear," I screamed out loud "it fell into the porridge." The child asked me what we could do about it and I said "Only you can save the fairy from drowning in the porridge. But it's an easy task. You just have to eat it. The fairy will be able to touch the ground with her feet and climb out of the bowl."

My friend's daughter ate all of her porridge. I told her that the fairy wanted to reward her with some healing magic and we started to tap while I quickly made up this rhyme:

There is a secret language that only fairies know.

It's about tapping some points in a row.

It's about rubbing a place where you're sore.

And a magic sentence with nine words or more.

The fairy asks, "Does it feel better a little?"

The child laughs "I feel as fit as a fiddle!"

I taught my friend the tapping sequence and her daughter was not only able to heal herself from her flu very quickly, but to use this tool to get rid of any stressful stuff she brought home from school. EFT can be used for bullying issues, fear of exams and more.

TESTIMONIALS

It was curiosity that drove me to make my appointment with Monika M. Lux. It wasn't until after I had my first treatment from Monika that I found out the meaning of Energy Healing or Energy Therapy. During this first counselling session Monika asked a few, but pertinent, questions that led to rediscovering old wounds.

These old wounds manifested in phobias for certain situations which led me to flee, for many years, unbearable to me, but perfectly normal social situations. Monika proceeded with an Emotional Freedom Technique (EFT), or Tapping as it is also known by.

At first, I wasn't sure what this was meant to do, but I followed her direction nevertheless, and shakily tapped along and repeated her words. After the tapping session was completed, Monika asked the question "How does it make you feel when you think of the social situation?" I thought and imagined, but felt neither agitation nor fear.

It has been four years, and to this date, the phobia, which used to send me running for so many years of my life, has never resurfaced.

I am utterly and deeply grateful to Monika and her ability to skillfully apply her psychological counselling knowledge and integrate it with the various energy treatment modalities she utilizes in her praxis.

Grace S., Lake Audy, Manitoba

As I continued losing body mass from Chemo, physical weakness became a serious problem at times. This was only compounded by a complete loss of appetite. Working on my meridians with Applied Kinesiology and EFT went along with restoring proper re-aligned strength and the determination to eat at all costs.

I have had digestions problems all my life which certainly contributed greatly to my current cancer issues. It was only after THREE sessions of re-aligning and balancing meridians that my whole digestive tract calmed right down. No more bloating, reflux, diarrhea etc. I was wondering "So, this is what it's like to feel "normal"? Wow!". I feel great and truly appreciate for the first time in my life having a HAPPY digestive system.

My physical body became more balanced and my mind became more balanced too – no irrational or fearful thoughts or worries.

I have learned EFT (Emotional Freedom Technique) with Monika in a group workshop in 2008. The basic recipe with positive affirmations from the sessions helped me move away from negative thoughts. "Down times" are fewer and less exhaustive. Tapping helps remind me that I can control my thoughts and it's very affirming. EFT has very much helped me control anxiety and worry especially in this past year of illness. And there's still a work in progress…

Jeff K., Erickson, Manitoba

Most workshops are inside a building with artificial light and in a big city. So, I appreciated it a lot to be able to sit outside for the whole day and enjoy the beauty of this unique place and the summer weather while learning about the Emotional Freedom Technique. The workshop was well organized and thanks to Monika's husband we had snacks in the morning, an awesome lunch and coffee in the afternoon. Everything was explained in a good understandable way, even for people who had no idea about Meridians or Energy healing. Monika is a very humorous instructor and intuitively creates a lot of metaphors which really made this workshop a very unique and vivid experience. In the afternoon, we worked on our personal issues on a one-to-one basis while the others could watch and learn how to dig deeper and discover the important aspects. I first thought it would be boring just to watch, but the way Monika was counselling the workshop members was such an exciting experience I would not have wanted to miss. Thanks to Monika and her husband for that great day.

Ashley W., Val Marie, Saskatchewan 2008

THE HISTORY OF TAPPING – FROM TFT TO CLINICAL EFT

TFT – Thought Field Therapy

- Developer: Dr. Roger Callahan
- Developed From: Ancient Meridian Energy Body Maps

Dr. Roger Callahan was the original founder of tapping techniques and the person who discovered that by tapping on meridian points on the body, people started to feel better.

The story goes that his first TFT patient "Mary" had an intense water phobia. After 18 months of conventional therapy with Callahan she would only reluctantly go near the edge of a swimming pool but no further, stating she had "awful feelings in her stomach."

Callahan then had the brain wave to ask Mary to think of the fear whilst tapping under her eye, which according to ancient energy body maps is linked to the stomach.

Without any other treatment, Mary suddenly exclaimed "It's gone! My fear of water, it's gone! I don't have those awful feelings in my stomach anymore!"

Over 30 years later, Mary is said to remain completely free of her phobia.

Callahan began experimenting with tapping meridian points and soon discovered that by bringing in other meridian points to tap on he could increase his success rate from an alleged 20% to 97%. His ideas were initially known as "Callahan Techniques" but later became Thought Field Therapy.

EFT - Emotional Freedom Techniques

- Developer: Gary Craig
- Developed From: TFT, NLP

Born April 13, 1940 in the US, Gary Craig is a Stanford Engineer, Ordained Minister and NLP Master Practitioner.

In 1991, Gary Craig became a student of Dr. Roger Callahan, founder of TFT, and over the next few years he began to devise EFT as a "one stop protocol" that would cover a multitude of problems by virtue of the concept of total redundancy.

"Rather than matching a problem to a tapping sequence, with EFT we only use one sequence and tap all the points for every problem. This is easier to learn and also takes the intuition out of the treatment flow making results more reliable to replicate." ~ Gary Craig

Another major difference between the two techniques is that TFT uses "muscle testing" as part of the treatment flow for gauging unconscious resistance, however Gary Craig decided to remove this as it is "loaded for potential inaccuracy", especially in the hands of beginners.

Branched out into:

Positive/Energy/Optimal/Faster EFT, **Matrix Re-imprinting (Karl Dawson), Tapping solution (Nick Ortner) etc.**

THE IMPORTANCE OF RELEASING EMOTIONAL BAGGAGE OR 95% UNCONSCIOUS VS 5% CONSCIOUS

Neuro-science found that whenever there is a conflict between reason and emotion, human beings will always side with emotion. Why? Because emotions are the language of the subconscious mind. And we are constantly controlled by emotional survival patterns and beliefs we absorbed like sponges, especially during the first 6 years of our childhood. If we want to life a fulfilled, happy and healthy life we have to be aware of our present emotions and release the supressed emotions of the past.

Often, we wonder why we reacted a certain way though we know better. Whatever worked as a survival pattern for us as children is still running as a subconscious program. But now it's time to replace it by a mature strategy.

Through emotional release we can heal most aspects of our life, physical, mental, emotional and spiritual.

When we get rid of our emotional baggage, we clear the way to manifest our true and highest potential.

CONTROL YOUR EMOTIONS - CONTROL YOUR REALITY

WATCH YOUR *EMOTIONS* BECAUSE THEY BECOME YOUR *THOUGHTS*

WATCH YOUR *THOUGHTS* BECAUSE THEY BECOME YOUR *WORDS*

WATCH YOUR *WORDS* BECAUSE THEY BECOME YOUR *ACTIONS*

WATCH YOUR *ACTIONS* BECAUSE THEY BECOME YOUR *HABITS*

WATCH YOUR *HABITS* BECAUSE THEY BECOME YOUR *CHARACTER*

WATCH YOUR *CHARACTER* BECAUSE IT BECOMES YOUR *DESTINY*

~ UNKNOWN

CORE LIMITING BELIEFS

Defectiveness Beliefs reflect a general sense that one is inherently flawed, incompetent, or inferior. Often times, people who maintain thoughts characteristic of a defective core belief withdraw from close relationships in fear that others may discover that there's something wrong with them at core. Examples of thoughts patterns characteristic of defectiveness include:

- I'm not good enough and/or I'm stupid/a failure
- I can't get anything right/I'm doing everything wrong
- I'm inferior and/or I'm worthless/insignificant/measure up to others (comparison)
- I'm nothing/useless
- I'm unattractive (ugly, fat, etc.)/there's something wrong with me
- I don't deserve anything good
- I'm always wrong (generalization)

Unlovable beliefs often cause people to make assumptions about the extent to which they belong and question whether they deserve love or can be loved. Individuals who believe they are unlovable may withdraw from relationships or maintain superficial companionships to avoid the suspected pain that will arise when they are inevitably rejected. Furthermore, the belief that one is unlovable can lead to significant feelings of loneliness even in the presence of others. Some thoughts related to an unlovable core belief include:

- I'm not lovable/unacceptable/unlikeable
- I'm always left out vs. I don't fit in anywhere
- I don't matter
- I'm not wanted/I'm not welcome
- I'm alone
- I'm uninteresting
- Nobody loves/wants me
- I'm bound to be rejected

Abandonment Beliefs create assumptions in people that they will lose anyone to whom they form an emotional attachment. Abandonment and unlovable core beliefs can often be related or even one and the same. Often times, those concerned with abandonment believe that people will ultimately leave, which will result in misery and loneliness. Consequently, people with abandonment beliefs almost constantly seek attention, reassurance and silence opinions out of fear that others will desert them in the presence of differing viewpoints. Examples of thoughts related to abandonment can include:

- People I love will leave me
- I will be abandoned if I love or care for something/someone
- I am uninteresting (and people will leave me because of it)
- If I assert myself, people will leave me
- I can't be happy if I'm on my own
- I'm bound to be rejected/abandoned/alone

Helplessness/Powerlessness Beliefs generally result in people assuming they lack control and cannot handle anything effectively or independently. Individuals who believe they are helpless often face difficulties making changes. Furthermore, a sense of powerlessness can cause people to become victims who try to over-control their environment. Some common thoughts reflecting helplessness/powerlessness core beliefs include:

- I'm helpless/powerless
- I'm out of control and I must have control to be okay
- I'm weak/vulnerable/needy
- I'm trapped and can't escape
- I do not measure up to others and/or I'm always number two/I always finish last
- I'm unsuccessful/I can't achieve
- I can't change and/or there's no way out
- I can't handle anything/I'm ineffective
- Other people will manipulate me and control my life
- If I experience emotions, I will lose control
- I can't do it and/or I'm a loser/failure
- I can't stand up for myself and/or I can't say "no"

Entitlement Beliefs are sometimes not entirely apparent. Generally, they reflect a belief related to specialness that causes individuals to make demands or engage in behaviors regardless of the effect on others. Those who maintain an entitlement core belief assume they are superior and deserve a lot of attention or praise. Often times, people develop an entitlement core belief to compensate for feeling defective or socially undesirable. Entitlement beliefs can lead to unreasonable demands that others meet your needs, rule-breaking, and resentment of successful others. Some entitlement-related beliefs include:

- If people don't respect me, I can't stand it
- I deserve a lot of attention and praise
- I'm superior/better than others (entitled to special treatment and privileges)
- If I don't excel, then I'm inferior and worthless/I'll just end up ordinary
- I am a very special person (and other people should treat me that way)
- I don't have to be bound by the rules that apply to other people
- If others don't respect me, they should be punished
- Other people should satisfy my needs
- People have no right to criticize me
- Other people don't deserve the good things that they get
- People should go out of their way for me
- People don't understand/get me (because I am special/brilliant/etc.)
- I can do no wrong/I'm always right

Caretaking/Responsibility/Self-Sacrifice Beliefs could be separated into independent categories, but they reflect similar beliefs and can be addressed as a group. Self-sacrifice beliefs refer to the excessive forfeit of one's own needs in the service of others. Individuals often feel guilty, and compensate by putting the needs of others ahead of their own. Such people often believe they are responsible for the happiness of others and apologize excessively. Responsible individuals may take pride in their diligence and dependability, without necessarily feeling a need to care for others or engage in self-sacrifice. People who maintain core beliefs rooted in caretaking, responsibility, or self-sacrifice may have felt overly responsible for family members in their youth. Related thoughts include:

- I have to do everything perfectly
- If I make a mistake, it means I'm careless/a failure/etc.
- If I've done something wrong, I have to make up for it, volunteering or helping others
- It's not okay to ask for help vs. I always have to be strong/tough
- I have to do everything myself
- If I don't do it, no one will
- I'm responsible for everyone and everything
- If I care enough, I can fix him/her/this
- I can't trust or rely on another person; if I do, they may hurt me (and I won't survive)
- People will betray me/people are untrustworthy

- My needs are not important/I shouldn't spend time taking care of myself
- When I see, that others need help, I have to help them
- I'm only worthwhile if I'm helping other people
- If I express negative feelings in a relationship, terrible things will happen
- I have to make people happy/If people are not happy it's my fault

The above core beliefs and related thoughts represent some common possibilities. Other core beliefs may relate to approval-seeking ("I'm only worth something if people like me"), autonomy ("if someone enters my world, I will have no freedom at all"), failure ("If I don't succeed, I'm worthless"), unwanted ("I don't belong anywhere"), etc.

CORE CAUSES WORKSHEET

While tapping on the side of your hand (formerly called "karate chop") to remove resistance and invite trauma to surface, explore areas of your life, core beliefs and trapped emotions.

1. What is your issue? Choose ONLY ONE specific issue at a time!

   o   Relationship / Sexuality
   o   Money / Work Place Challenges
   o   Purpose
   o   Transition / Change
   o   Health / Body
   o   Peak Performance / Success
   o   Grief / ANY Loss (health, work, pet, loved one)
   o   Other

   _____

2. What are the trapped emotions associated with your issue?

   o   Fear / Being Afraid
   o   Feeling (Mortally) Terrified
   o   Anger / Rage
   o   Anxiety
   o   Overwhelmed
   o   Burned-out
   o   Depressed / Frustrated
   o   Unsafe / Life-threatening
   o   Deeply Hurt
   o   Alone
   o   Sadness / Grief

o   Stuck / Frozen

o   Resentful / Vengeful

o   Betrayed

o   Not Heard / Misunderstood

o   Attacked

o   Heartbroken

o   Stupid

o   Embarrassed

o   Humiliated

o   Unloved

o   Unworthy

o   Hopeless

o   Broken

o   Helpless / Trapped

o   Disconnected

o   Addicted (food, drugs)

o   Hateful

o   Used

o   Shame / Ashamed

o   Manipulated

o   Incapable

o   Dirty / Evil

o   Guilty

o   Embarrassed

---

3.   What's your negative "self-talk" about this issue? (Choose from this list or Core Limiting Beliefs)

o   I'm not good enough. / I'm stupid

o   It's impossible to heal.

o   I don't have what it takes.

o   What will they think?

o   I'm scared to fail.

o   If I'm successful people will hate me

o   Rich people are greedy.

o   I'm afraid of responsibility

o   I will lose love, appreciation and attention.

o   I will never trust again.

o   I am unworthy of love.

o   In the end, I'm left alone.

o   I'm not ready yet.

o   Nobody helps me! / I'm to proud to ask for help. / I have to do it by myself.

o   I'm ugly / unattractive.

o   I'm TOO …

o   I should have … (but now it's too late).

o   Life is not fair to me. / I don't deserve …

o   I'm afraid of being seen.

o   I can't be heard.

o   I'll be punished.

o   I'm the victim!

o   I will never forgive...

o   My needs don't matter.

o   I'm a burden.

o   Everything is out of my control!

o   Life is too hard!

o   I'll never succeed. / I'm a born loser.

o   I don't deserve happiness.

o   'm stuck forever...

o   I just want to die.

o   Other (please specify)

_____

4.   What beliefs did you learn during your upbringing? (Example: "If you don't go to church you'll burn in hell.")

Please specify:

_____

_____

_____

5. Who do you blame or hold responsible for this issue, (even if it's not actually their fault)?

   o   Myself
   o   (Step) Mother or (Step) Father
   o   Sister(s) or Brother(s)
   o   Grandma or Grandpa
   o   Aunt or Uncle
   o   Cousin(s)
   o   Friend(s)
   o   Child Care
   o   Teacher / Coach
   o   Religion / Church / God
   o   Neighbor
   o   Husband / Wife
   o   Child / Children
   o   Society/Mentality
   o   Karma

   _____

6. Who in your family modeled similar attitudes and feelings? (Could you have picked up or inherited feelings, thoughts and beliefs from someone you were around as a child?) One of your:

   o   (Step) Parents
   o   Sibling(s)
   o   Grandparents
   o   People who raised me.
   o   Other (please specify)

   _____

   _____

7. Where do you feel this in your body? (For example: It may be a pressure in your head or a tension in your stomach.)

   o   My entire body
   o   Head
   o   Face

o   Eyes
o   Ears
o   Neck
o   Throat
o   Shoulders
o   Arms
o   Hands
o   Chest
o   Heart
o   Back
o   Stomach
o   Hips
o   Legs
o   Knees
o   Other (please specify)

_____

_____

8.   What benefit(s) do you think you're receiving by holding on to this issue?

o   Protection
o   Teaching a lesson
o   Punishing myself
o   My suffering hurts them.
o   Proving something
o   Attention/Love
o   Other (please specify)

_____

_____

How would this issue or belief look like if you'd created a picture/collage of it?

Give it a shape (abstract or a concrete), object or geometric design, whatever first comes into your mind. Is it black and white or color, small or large in size, just a scribble, some doodling?

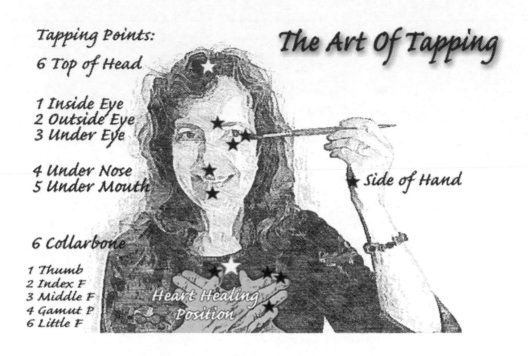

Tapping Points:

6 Top of Head

1 Inside Eye
2 Outside Eye
3 Under Eye

4 Under Nose
5 Under Mouth

★ Side of Hand

6 Collarbone

1 Thumb
2 Index F
3 Middle F
4 Gamut P
6 Little F

Heart Healing Position

The Art Of Tapping

Emotional Pain Scale

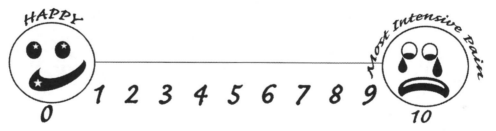

HAPPY

Most Intensive Pain

0   1   2   3   4   5   6   7   8   9   10

"Even though I'm feeling ... I deeply and completely accept, love and forgive myself"

"I choose to release the trauma and pattern behind the blocked emotion of ... that no longer serves me in a positive and productive way."

Even though I STILL have... Remaining ...

22

BASIC PROCEDURE

Assume Heart Healing Posture (HHP) and take three deep breaths, in and out.

Say the set-up statement and tap the

Side Of Hand Point SOH (Small Intestine) or rub Sore Spots (neuro-lymphatic points) to identify and correct psychological reversal

Take a deep breath in and out before moving on to the next treatment point.

Then continue to:

1. **Top of the Eyebrow TOE (Bladder – Fear/Feeling Trapped)**

2. **Corner of the Eye COE (Gall Bladder – Depression/Resentment/Indecisiveness)**

3. **Under Eye UE (Stomach – Worry/Betrayal/Distrust)**

4. **Under Nose UN (Governing Vessel – Feeling Inferior/Disconnection)**

5. **Under Mouth UM (Central Vessel – Shame/Embarrassment/Bitter Humiliation)**

More Points:

Under Arm UA (Spleen – Lack of Control/Obsessive Thoughts/Hopelessness)

Under breast or rib point UB (Liver – Anger/Aggressiveness/Envy/Vengeance)

6. **Tap on Top Of Head TOH (Governing Vessel: anchoring/central nervous system) and Under Collarbone UC (Kidneys – Death Fear/Terror/Dread) at the same time + switch hands**

7. **Assume the HHP (Heart Healing Position) for a moment of silent reflection. Take six deep breaths, in and out.**

Check your pain level on the scale. (Subjective Units of Distress – SUD Level)

THE 9 GAMUT PROCEDURE

has a very useful function. ***It integrates both sides of the brain.*** It only takes about a minute to perform and you can use it in the middle of a tapping sequence to increase the effectiveness of EFT or ***to get you 'unstuck' if you are not making progress***.

Start with a round of tapping in the usual way.

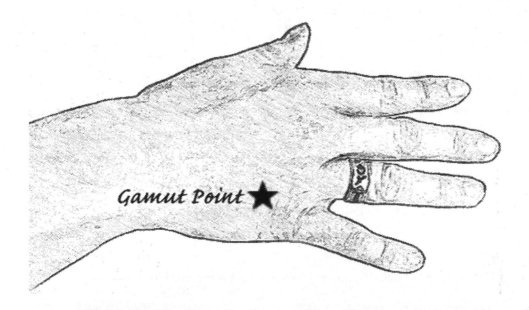

Gamut Point ★

Then locate the Gamut point on the top of the left hand, about an inch below the web between the small finger and the ring finger. Gently keep tapping on this point and focus on the problem while you do the following, without moving your head:

1. **Thumb T (Lungs – Grief/Sadness/Cravings/Addictions)**

2. **Index Finger IF (Large Intestine – Rigidness/Defensiveness/Stubbornness)**

3. **Middle Finger MF (Circulation Sex/Heart Protector – Rejection/Abandonment)**

4. **Little Finger LF (Heart – Shock/Guilt/Lack of Emotion/Holding on to Hurt & Pain)**

5. **While tapping the Gamut* GP (Triple Warmer – Confused Thinking/Instability)**

CLOSE YOUR EYES then OPEN YOUR EYES

LOOK HARD DOWN TO YOUR RIGHT then LOOK HARD DOWN TO YOUR LEFT

MOVE YOUR EYES IN A CLOCKWISE CIRCLE then MOVE THEM IN AN

ANTI-CLOCKWISE CIRCLE

HUM A FEW SECONDS of any song ("Happy Birthday" works well)

Now COUNT OUT LOUD (1-2-3-4-5)

HUM a few seconds again

*The Gamut point is also called "Brain Balancer" and it's *the one to tap for Hormonal Imbalance or symptoms like Hot Flashes*

AFFIRMATION TAPPING FOR EACH MERIDIAN

Tap on the related meridian point and say the affirmation out loud. Take a deep breath after each sentence. Start with side of hand and end with baby finger. You may as well hold the fingers (Jin Shin Jyutsu – Japanese Self-Help Technique) and say the affirmation.

	Affirmations	**Meridian**
SOH	I feel warm, nurtured, loved and connected.	Small Intestine
TOE	I am in harmony, at peace and fully alive.	Bladder
COE	I reach out with tolerance and release all judgment.	Gall bladder
UE	I trust my gut feelings and the mystery of life.	Stomach
UN	I am deeply grounded and standing tall.	Governing
UM	I am clear, centered and safe.	Central
UA	I have faith and confidence in my future.	Spleen
UB	I am kind, loving and forgiving to myself.	Liver
UC	I step forward with courage. I open my heart to love.	Kidneys
T	I breathe in humbleness and breathe out faith.	Lungs
IF	I am relaxed and generous. I support my heart & soul needs.	Circulation-Sex
MF	I surrender and let go of the cords attached to the past.	Large Intestine
GP	I honor my inner Warrior; I am ready to overcome any issue.	Triple Warmer
LF	I love myself for who I am; my heart is filled with forgiveness.	Heart

HHP: Take 6 healing breaths

You may muscle test if there's a meridian that most needs your attention (page 26) and look at its meaning (page 15, 16). Intuitively draw a picture of the issue (example: governing vessel = feeling inferior). Do you remember an incident as a child when you felt inferior? Tap on whatever comes up when you look at the drawing. Release through breathing.

EXPRESSIVE ART THERAPY – THE LANGUAGE OF SYMBOLS AND METAPHORS

Language is originally and essentially nothing but a system of signs or symbols, which denote real occurrences, or their echo in the human soul. Symbolic or nonlinear thinking is holistic, right-brain oriented; it is complementary to logical, linear, left-brain thinking.

Chinese proverb: "One picture is worth ten thousand words."

Deep metaphors start developing since our birth, and are shaped with our social environment. In this sense, metaphors are involved with language, emotion, and our innate abilities. Highly, metaphors work unconsciously, still they are deep. Metaphors are essential ways in language of defining ideas. Our conceptual system, the very way that we perceive our world, is fundamentally metaphorical in nature.

Metaphors analyse two objects and collate them by suggesting that two objects are similar to each other, as well as they are quite unlike. The way that metaphors are used, they allow obtaining information from a fresh sight, and improving new learning methods. Visual metaphors are a concept that demonstrate how the visual imagination is systematized by meanings through culture and experiences. Forms, icons and symbols may represent different meanings and seem in different appearance as visual metaphors, but they express the same influence across cultures. We make metaphors to use as a reason to understand the concepts that are based on our experiences and actions. A sound, sometimes a picture or a word may represent the feelings and ideas, and how we perceive the concept metaphorically. Metaphors are usually based on emotions, even with verbal or visual.

Metaphor speaks to the heart and it is only with the heart that one can see rightly*. For this reason, metaphor has long been the language of mystics, spiritual teachers, poets, storytellers and other expressive artists. Metaphor is a heart-tool that helps us explore the ideas, forces and powers that lie behind our rational thought.

*In Antoine de Saint-Exupéry's book *The Little Prince* we learn a simple secret from the fox:

"And now here is my secret, a very simple secret: It is only with the heart that one can see rightly; what is essential is invisible to the eye."

THE POWER OF ART THERAPY

Art Therapy combines visual art and psychotherapy in a creative process using the created image as a foundation for self-exploration and understanding. Thoughts and feelings often reach expression in images rather than words. Through the use of art therapy, feelings and inner conflicts can be projected into visual form. In the creative act, conflict is re-experienced, resolved and integrated. - The B.C. Art Therapy Association

Art therapy improves self-awareness and self-esteem. Art therapy is very beneficial for people struggling with:

- Life transitions
- Relationship issues – Divorce – Separation – Co-dependency etc.
- Addictions
- Depression – Anxiety – Post Traumatic Stress Disorder – Grief & Loss
- Anxiety – Phobias – Eating Disorder

The Marriage of EFT And Expressive Art Therapy Gives Birth To "The Art Of Tapping"

Developed by Monika Marguerite Lux during counseling work with teens in transition on social phobias, different anxieties, traumatic childhood experiences, first grief, PTSD etc.

Sometimes we live our lives like puzzle pieces turned upside down - only showing the world our gray sides. Then along comes life, and it starts flipping them over, showing to us and the world more than just the outline of who we are - it shows us the colors. If we can start to turn more over and put them together, we can see the picture of who we really are emerge. ~Manifest~

While many of us may find it hard to put our feelings about a tough experience from the past into words, drawing a picture or piecing together a collage can help us convey our sadness, regret or anger clearly—giving us the much-needed chance to release those negative emotions. Many counselors find art therapy just as effective (and sometimes even more so) as other practices that help us uncover different aspects of our personalities and cope with challenges or traumas.

EMOTIONAL RELEASE EXERCISES

Journaling & Drawing – The Puzzle Of Life

Take a journal or piece of paper and write a story about a chapter in your life that still "puzzles" you.

Start tapping on the side of your hand:

Even though I still don't understand… I deeply and completely love, accept and forgive myself. Maybe it's not necessary to understand, but trust my inner healer to show me the way.

Write down whatever surfaces: emotions, thoughts, beliefs

Draw a picture or symbol for this chapter in your life. Your subconscious will understand what it is all about.

Tap on the side of your hand:

Even though there is this circle, square… / even though it has this … color, shape and I don't know what it means, I deeply and completely love, accept and forgive myself.

Even though there is this emotion of… surfacing now, I deeply and completely love, accept and forgive myself.

Tap on the top of your head and your heart:

I choose to let it go!

Switch hands:

It's safe to let it go!

Tap your wrists/pulse points together.

Assume heart healing position:

I'm at peace!

Take 6 deep healing breaths and imagine how you release this chapter of your past through your feet into the EARTH.

Non-Dominant Hand Drawing – Conversation With Your Higher Self

Drawing with your non-dominant hand allows you to silence your inner critic.

When you write with your dominant hand (regardless of whether you are left- or right-handed), you access the logical, linear, verbal part of your mind. This is the everyday mind, and it dominates our culture.

Switching hands activates what we think of as the right brain – the creative, holistic, subconscious, intuitive brain – that tends to be underdeveloped and underutilized.

The right brain is not concerned with protecting our ego and preserving the status quo. It's more about reflecting the truth as we understand it. The subconscious is constantly absorbing and processing information, sending up hunches, flashes of insight, gut feelings. By switching the pen to your nondominant hand, it's like you find a way to surface this hidden stream of nonverbal intelligence and translate it to words on the page.

Set your intention to work on a specific issue or traumatic event in your life. Let the most important aspect about it be downloaded from your subconscious mind and sent through your arm, to your hand, to the pen and onto the paper in front of you into a spontaneous movement, drawing, scribble or doodling. *Your pen is NOT supposed to leave the paper. The movement is fast and short.*

Leave your hand on the scribble, gaze at it with soft eyes. Ask your subconscious mind to bring up a memory from the past related to your spontaneous scribble and write it down with all the details you can remember. Look at the core emotions (page 10/2.) Write down how you felt (for example abandoned, not heard, rejected etc.)

Close your eyes and imagine your younger self, just after the traumatic event. Acknowledge your emotions. You had every right to feel them. Take the hands of this beautiful child, that had to endure so much pain and with a firm voice tell it: "I am very sorry for leaving you alone. I acknowledge your suffering. You had the right to feel the way you felt after this incident. Please forgive me as I forgive myself. I love you deeply and I accept myself completely for who I am. Thank you for helping me release and gaining back my power." Repeat while tapping on the side of your hand and top of the head & heart points. Release while breathing deeply and assuming the Heart Healing Posture.

Two-Hand Drawings – Live Chat

Have two pieces of paper in front of you. Attach them to the table with some adhesive tape. Now, you can do two different exercises and then tap on whatever comes up.

Take a pencil in each hand and draw some abstract lines and shapes with both of your hands at the same time. Abstract drawing means drawing with artistic inspiration but without specific intentions in mind. Let your hands be moved totally by the creative spirit.

Reflect on how this feels to you. How are your hands communicating with each other? What is the communication about? Did you have a certain issue in mind? Did a certain issue come up while you were drawing? Are your hands circling in the same or opposite direction? Are they playing together as a team or are there some difficulties within the communication? How does this activity make you feel? What emotions can you sense? What does flowing mean to you? Is the movement of one or both hands interrupted? Did one hand move faster than the other?

Write the answers in your journal and start tapping through the sequence. Example: "Even though my left hand moved faster than my right hand, I deeply and completely love, accept and forgive myself. I acknowledge that in this moment one hand moves faster than the other. It might be different tomorrow and I don't have to know why. I trust my higher self to guide me to heal myself and find happiness."

Again, take your pencils. Just this time, you ask a question with your right hand on any issue that's bothering you and answer with your left hand. Remember, it's about abstract drawing. Question and Answer will appear in front of you as a pattern, lines and shapes.

You are going to tap on the answer. Example: "Even though I look at the lines and might not understand consciously, my higher self knows how to decipher the subconscious code and I trust the process. I deeply and completely love, accept and forgive myself. I acknowledge and honor the answer and all the emotions that come with it. It's time to move on. It's time to re-create. It's time to let go what no longer serves me."

Ideograms & Metaphors – Healing Symbols From The Sacred Place Of Your Heart

"The soul never thinks without an image." ~ Aristotle

Universal shapes have significant psychological and mythological meanings embedded in our minds. Life is art and stories have shapes that support our very own processes of growth. The language of the unconscious and of the deep inner self is comprised of imagery (shapes), metaphors and feelings. We construct our world through metaphor. We can only conceptualise by making comparisons between different realms of experience. A metaphor shows us one thing as another, and in doing so extends the way we see the world, also often refreshing and enlivening our perception. In oral and written language, using the medium of picture imagery, metaphor speaks directly to our imaginative faculties, bypassing our rational brain. Such metaphoric byways and pathways enable us to explore the ideas, forces, and powers that lie behind or beyond our rational thought and helps us in overcoming the limitations of our fixed categories. Ideograms are the written physical language between you and your subconscious mind. Each ideogram is a symbol for an idea, a concept, or a thing. We refer to the ideas, concepts and things that ideograms represent as gestalts.

Again, with your non-dominant hand, fill part or all of the page, moving more rapidly until you reach the point of letting go of control and surrender to the actual message of your subconscious, creating a picture of shapes melting into each other until the movement comes to an end.

Stay with this stillness and emptiness, gazing at the picture in front of you. Put the pen aside and start tapping on whatever comes up.

For example: "Even though there is this circle and it feels uncomfortable, threatening, unknown…, I deeply and completely love, accept and forgive myself." "This line, it feels abrasive. This triangle pokes into my heart. When I look at the picture, anger surfaces. etc."

It doesn't have to make sense to your left brain. The Art Of Tapping is a right brain process. You tap along with all your sensual perceptions: visual, auditory, kinesthetic, olfactory, gustatory. If there were colors, what would you see? If there were sounds, what would you hear?

In fact, you may take some water colors, colored pencils or crayons and color your scribble (nowadays, that's called "Zentangle"). How does it look like when it's colored? What colors did you use? Do they make you feel good?

Perhaps there was a shift happening while you were painting and coloring. Something may have changed from feeling uncomfortable to being at peace, looking at your unique piece of art. Summon the release and courage to surrender the old and emerge like the Phoenix from the ashes of your past.

This is a spontaneously drawn scribble Rule: Trust the reactions of your body without exception. Your body always tells the truth. Trust it. And always trust the very first reaction. Never anticipate what your Universal Ideogram should look like, just let your body give you the shape, as quickly as possible.

The ideogram is an amazing phenomenon. It holds the taste, color, temperature, emotions, activity - everything there is to know about your issue, traumatic event, anxiety etc. in a very small package.

You may also try to tap the EFT points with your right hand while moving the pen with your left hand or vice versa.

Time Line – Make Your Visions Come True

I use this NLP technique for eliminating obstacles and challenges, by travelling along the timeline and into the future, getting unstuck with the help of EFT and reaching whatever goal was set. It is a really powerful process.

Draw two pictures:

1st picture	2nd picture
How I view myself now	How I would like to view myself (living my full potential, being my true self)
Situation now	Project's Goal: weight loss, higher position, promotion etc.

Put the pictures on the floor as far away from each other as the size of the room allows. Imagine there is an invisible path between them (you can also put a rope between or draw a line).

Step into today's picture, close your eyes and become aware of the energy field.

Then step into the future picture and compare.

Become aware of your posture. Is there any tension in one of the fields? Are you standing taller in one of the fields? Are your hands open or closed tight in fists? Are you tempted to fold your arms tightly across your chest in one of the fields, while you feel open and relaxed in the other? What about your other senses? Are there different sounds within the fields? Put a paper next to each field and write down what's different.

To start the process, step into today's field. Slowly take your first step towards your future self or the goal you set. Can you move forward? Is something slowing you down? Is something stopping you completely from moving on? Whenever there's an obstacle and your subconscious doesn't give you any clue, start self-muscle testing. (see chapter following the exercises)

- When was the first time I had this special emotion, stopping me from moving forward and reaching my goal?
- Inherited through generations (family history)? Before birth, during conception? During pregnancy (in the womb) During birth?
- Age 0-7 – the 'imprint' period (we are like a sponge and absorb everything and go through our first experiences of all kinds of emotions).
- Age 7–14 – the 'modelling period' (we tend to have 'heroes' and role models).
- Age 14–21 is the 'socialising period' (we begin establishing relationships)
- Who was involved? Parents? Siblings? Relatives? Partners?
- At age 0-5, 5-10 etc.?

    Trust your conscious mind and accept the first thing that comes up (this is usually the accurate one).

- Can I release it now?

Start tapping on the side of your hand. "Even though there was … (this incident), I deeply and completely love, accept and forgive myself. And I choose to release NOW all that no longer serves me in a positive and productive way." Tap through the sequence "I acknowledge this emotion. It was alright to feel it then. But now I don't have to hold on to it anymore. I choose to release/ it's good to release/I'm ready to release etc." Take 6 breaths in heart healing position and self-muscle test if it's gone.

EMOTIONAL EMPOWERMENT EXERCISES

The theory behind tapping is that negative emotions disrupt the flow of energy through the meridians, creating disharmony and imbalances in the body. The spoken statements keep your mind focused on the incident and its difficult memories while the tapping releases the associated blocked energy. The combination of tapping on specific points along with verbal statements gently realigns the body's energy system and natural flow. I found that each emotional release creates a bit of a void that needs to be filled with a sense of safety, love and personal empowerment.

Your Safe Place

Think about a place where you would feel absolutely safe and loved. How would it look like? It can be a place in nature (lake, river, ocean, forest, mountain, meadow etc.), a fantasy place ("Sacred Bubble", "Magic Shell" etc.), a room in a house that only exists in your dreams… Choose your favorite art technique (watercolours, crayons, markers, pencils etc.) and draw or paint this safe place. It's YOUR place! It's always with you in your heart. You can always return to it, in order to recover, recharge and revive.

Ask yourself: What colour, what smell, what sound, what taste, what feeling suggests stability and safety?

Tap through the sequence, looking at your finished picture: Even though I sometimes feel scared and alone, I deeply and completely love, accept and forgive myself. But there's a place, a place of safety, a place filled with unconditional love… There's this beautiful color _____. I can smell _____. I hear _____. I taste _____. When I touch _____ (water, grass, walls etc.) it feels _____ (warm, smooth, like silk etc.) This place will be in my heart forever and I can return at any given time and relax for a while… recharge my batteries… focusing on my breath. Breathe in and say/think "slow down", breathe out and say/think "relax".

"Breathing in, I calm body and mind. Breathing out, I smile. Dwelling in the present moment I know this is the only moment." ~ Thich Nhat Hanh

Unconditional Love

What does unconditional love look like? When did you feel loved? How did it feel? How were your 5 senses involved in the experience? Draw how unconditional love would look like if you had to express it on a piece of paper through art.

Tap through the sequence with everything you see in your picture (those flowing lines, the fusing colours, the round shape etc.). If a positive memory pops up in your mind include it in the tapping. Think gratitude! Thank this unique friend or family member who loves and accepts you just the way you are.

YOUR Personal Tree Of Life

Draw yourself as a tree of life and then reflect (use your journal) and tap on how deep you want your roots to grow, how flexible your trunk should be to withstand the storms of life, how far you want your branches to reach out, what kind of green dress you'd like to wear and what flowers, fruits or cones you would like to give birth to.

How does the completed picture look like? Is there something missing? What's surrounding the tree (grass, flowers, bushes, clouds, sun)? Are some parts bigger, more detailed or colourful than others?

How do you feel about the tree as a whole? Tap on what's coming to mind. If you like to add something after the tapping, just do it. Let your tree grow more and more beautiful and whole. Don't worry or overthink the process! Trust your subconscious intelligence to understand and guide you on your healing journey.

Personal Achievement

Draw an experience where you did something you didn't think you could do.

We all have accomplished something we didn't even dare to think about.

My story: "I remember that I had never done a presentation in front of people till I was forty-one. I happened to be at work and talked to a customer. She was the president of the Rotary Club and seemed very interested in energy healing. After a while she asked me if I would hold a speech about this interesting topic. I felt highly honored and accepted. At home, I was wondering how I was going to do it. I just had immigrated to Manitoba and my English wasn't that good. In addition to that, I had no idea how to do a presentation or deliver a speech.

I created an energy field representing my father (systemic constellation) because he was incredible at speaking freely in front of any audience. I stepped into the field and felt already empowered. Then I tapped on all the fearful emotions that popped into my head. I felt very calm but still insecure, especially about my English. I visited a tutor at the career center and we put a speech together. I still had one week to work on my fears and insecurity. After tapping for the next three days, I ripped apart the pre-fabricated speech and wrote it in my own words.

Everything went very well. Although there were over twenty people in the room I stayed calm, held eye-contact with my audience and spoke fluently.

I was not just rewarded with an incredible applause but also with a job at Royal Bank of Canada. This had only been 6 months after my immigration."

After drawing the picture, tap on everything that made you feel good about your achievement.

For me it would be: accomplishment, courage, reputation, self-esteem, strength, to be seen and heard, still hearing the applause, feeling people are interested in my work, the thrill of presenting and speaking that came with this first experience, the belief that I can overcome any obstacle in my life with EFT etc.

DANCE AND/OR MOVEMENT THERAPY

helps individuals achieve emotional, cognitive, physical, and social integration. Beneficial for both physical and mental health, dance/movement therapy can be used for stress reduction, disease prevention, and mood management. In addition, the physical component offers increased muscular strength, coordination, mobility, and decreased muscular tension. dance/movement therapy can be used with all populations and with individuals, couples, families, or groups. In general, dance therapy promotes self-awareness, self-esteem, and a safe space for the expression of feelings.

Freestyle dancing helps people get out of their heads and reconnect with their hearts, intuition, community and inner wisdom. It is about moving authentically, gaining self-awareness and allowing emotions to surface and leave the body in a natural way. The goal is to feel grounded and at peace at the end of the session.

1. Exercise

Think about an event or memory that caused you emotional disturbance. Write it down in your journal or on a piece of paper.

Tap on each of the core feelings coming up while thinking about the memory. Finally tap on the side of your hand: "Even though all those emotions had been with me for quite a while, I deeply and completely love, accept and forgive myself." Tap on top of the head and heart points (switching hands and repeating the statement): "I choose to release them with the following dance."

With the goal of letting go in your mind, put on some music. Don't think about your movements. Trust your body's knowledge and let the music and its rhythm move you. You may close your eyes for a short while. Make your movements big, involving your whole body. Express your feelings with your arms, hands, legs, feet and posture. If you are angry, stomp your feet on the floor or punch the air as in shadow boxing. If you are sad, let those tears roll down your cheeks and keep on dancing. If you feel anxious include empowering expansive poses (for example the winner pose) and reflect on how they make you feel.

After the dance sit down and silently tap through the sequence again, ending with your six breathes in heart position.

Slow Dance of Awareness

Put on some meditative music and move through the room as slowly as you can and with awareness of sensations from muscles and joints, postural sway and stability, and any emotional feelings, that these movements bring up for you.

Reflect: Do I have to slow down on my dance of life? Have I found my very own pace and rhythm? Are my movements flowing smoothly or rather disrupted and unbalanced? Am I taking big or small steps? How does it affect my movement when I open my arms? How am I impacted by different movements of arms and legs or my whole body? Is there anything that stops one of my movements from unfolding?

After the music stops, write down whatever comes up and tap on it. You may also draw a picture (Mandala) of your experience and tap on the picture.

2. Exercise

Go for a nature walk. Think about something that weighs you down and tap on it while walking (emotional release through movement). If you feel angry push some dirt or gravel with your feet or just stomp on the ground with your boots. You may also take stones and throw them into a river.

Take responsibility for your feelings and acknowledge them. That's the only way to gain the power to release them successfully.

Place your attention on the part of your body where you're holding the trauma, and with every exhalation of your breath, have an intention of letting it go.

For the next 10 breaths, just feel the painful sensation leaving your body.

It may help to make an audible tone, to sing, to dance or to run. After your walk, you may experiment with writing out your emotions on pieces of paper and then ritually burn them and offer the ashes to the winds.

Feel the anger leaving your body. Now drop down into the sacred place of your heart, the very center of love and compassion. As you breathe deeply, allow your heart to open. Visualize and feel suffused with the light of love and compassion. Feel its healing power, accept it, own it! Allow this light to penetrate your body, soul and your entire being and let it create a deep sense of peace and protection within and all around you.

SELF MUSCLE TESTING - THE SWAY TEST

Do I need to know more? How to self muscle-test.

Before you start: Cook's Hookup will hook up the electromagnetic energy your body and brain run on, so it's flowing smoothly again and you won't be overwhelmed by fuzzy thinking.

Cross one ankle over the other.

Cross the same arm over the other. Open your hands and clap the palms together. Join the fingers together and bring the hands under and up to the chest.

Place the tongue on the roof of the mouth.

Stay in this position for a few minutes, breathing deeply and slowly. Switch legs and hands.

Stand straight with your knees unlocked and your feet pointing directly forward. Relax your body with your hands down at your sides.

Now you are ready to perform an accuracy check: First make a statement or hold a thought in your head you know to be true for your "YES" response.

Then make a statement that can only be answered with a clear "NO".

Sense the response of your body for each — you should either feel yourself being gently pulled forward for a "yes" response, or repelled back signaling it's not true or your body is not in resonance with that, which would be a "no" response.

Now, you can test if you need to know more about the issue on hand or if you can already release it through the tapping process. If you subconscious tells you, you need to know more, you can ask the following questions:

When did this issue start? Between birth and 5? 5 and 10? And so on. If you get the answer "between birth and 5", you can ask for the exact age: with 5? With 6? And so on.

You may also ask who was involved: My father, my mother, a teacher, a school mate, a partner etc.

If something pops into your head, you may ask: Is this the incident that has to be dealt with and released?

It may take some practice to be accurate and consistent. Just keep at it though and you'll find a whole new way to communicate with your body through muscle testing.

With this technique, you can even test food sensitivities. Place the substance you are testing in one hand and close your fist over it. Hold this hand up to your heart center, which is your thymus gland. Then place your other hand over the first one.

State: "This is good for my body."

Become still, centered, close your eyes, take a deep breath, release it and let go. After a few moments, you become aware of your body either being pulled forward or falling backwards.

EFT FOR BABIES, CHILDREN AND PETS

DON'T Necessarily Tap ON Your Animal!!

When people first find out about EFT for babies, children and pets, they immediately think that it is about tapping. But it might be very upsetting for babies and animals alike when they are tapped on AND your child might not be at home when experiencing a traumatic event. So, you tap on yourself to make the changes happen. That's when surrogate tapping comes very handy.

And there is a benefit for you too, called "borrowing benefit" in EFT. It simply means you heal yourself because you might have had a similar experience in your own childhood.

How Does Surrogate/Proxy Tapping Work?

When you focus your attention on an animal, you connect your energy system with theirs.

When you keep the focus of your attention on a specific aspect of that energy system (a problem, disease, behaviour, state of mind and so on) and you change YOUR system by tapping on the points, YOU ARE ALSO CHANGING THEIRS through the energetic connection (phenomenon of morphic resonance).

This was originally discovered when a lady, distraught because she was sitting by the side of her premature baby's incubator and unable to touch him, treated herself for the baby's problems and the baby responded by breathing more easily and slower, and finding from somewhere the will to live and to fight on more strongly than before.

Since then, thousands of people all over the world have been absolutely astonished to find that by tapping on themselves whilst holding another living being's problems in their mind, they can make changes without touching them or even being in the same room.

1. **Focus Your Intention: Tuning In**

Think about the animal and what specifically you would like to release, soothe or change.

2. **Make A Statement Of Intent: The Set Up**

Find a phrase or a sentence that describes the problem succinctly and clearly to you. For pets for example, you can say, "Tom has this terrible allergy." or "Sam never stops barking." or, "This brown horse is distressed." if you don't know the animals' name.

3. **Tap The EFT Round(s) as often as needed** until you really feel good and positive within.

Try it on EVERYTHING:

- training problems
- health problems
- relationship problems like jealousy, aggression
- attention seeking behaviours, repetitive behaviour disturbances
- stress and nervousness, fears, phobias, self esteem, unhappiness, resentfulness, lack of social skills
- sadness, depression, lack of joy in life
- pain, discomfort, disturbance, disease, allergies, past traumas, mistreatment, mishandling, misuse

DAILY SELF-CARE - FORGIVENESS PROCEDURE BY IYANLA VANZANT

Tap 7 times on each meridian point while repeating out loud
either the statements below or your reminder phrases.

ROUND 1

Top of Eyebrow: I feel guilty and ashamed about some of the things that I've thought, said, and done.

Corner of Eye: And the way that I have hurt myself and other people.

Under Eye: I feel so guilty about some things I have done and not done.

Under Nose: I feel so ashamed about certain things I have said and done.

Under mouth: I feel embarrassed about things I have said and done or not said and not done.

Collarbone: Someplace inside of me, it feels as if I am not a very nice person or a good person.

Under arm: I feel as if I'm not even worth forgiving.

Under breast: I am learning how to forgive other people, but I can't seem to forgive myself.

Wrists: I am carrying around so much unforgiveness.

Top of Head: I feel so bad about myself, so unforgiving.

ROUND 2

Top of Eyebrow: What if I stop beating myself up?

Corner of Eye: What if it's time to start letting go of the guilt, shame, and unforgiveness?

Under Eye: What if I acknowledge that everything is a lesson and that I was just doing the best I could?

Under Nose: What if I let go of the feeling that I can't forgive myself?

Under Mouth: What if making that small choice starts the forgiveness process?

Collarbone: What if I forgive myself a little at a time so that I feel safe and comfortable?

Under arm: What if I release all feelings of guilt, shame, and blame?

Under breast: What if I give myself permission to transform my unforgiveness and self-judgment into peace and freedom?

Wrists: What if nothing happens?

Top of Head: What if something does happen, something like I forgive myself?

ROUND 3

Top of Eyebrow: It feels as if I am ready to release all forms of unforgiveness toward myself.

Corner of Eye: It feels like I am opening to the possibility of forgiving myself totally and completely.

Under Eye: It feels like I am already forgiven by everyone for everything.

Under Nose: This forgiveness is very powerful.

Under Mouth: I am tapping into the power of forgiveness right now.

Collarbone: I am much more open and much better now.

THE ART OF TAPPING

Under arm: I am open to forgiving myself for creating or choosing experiences that require self-forgiveness.

Under breast: I have learned my lessons and release the need to repeat them.

Wrists: I allow my mind and heart to experience total and complete forgiveness of myself for everything.

Crown of Head: I know that everything has happened for my highest and greatest good.

Thank you! Thank you! Thank you!

ROUND 4 Now it's your turn! Tap on each meridian point speaking out loud what you are grateful for!

I am grateful / thankful for my wonderful mind and body / health / partner / home / friends etc.

EFT TAPPING FOR GRIEF

"We never lose our loved ones. The accompany us; they don't disappear from our lives. We are merely in different rooms." — *Paulo Coelho*, *Aleph*

SET THE INTENTION TO HEAL and remember to drink enough water before, during and after the tapping!

Tap on the side of hand and say:

"I have the intention to release the sadness and grief from my heart."

When you think about your loss, what emotion do you feel? Where do you feel that emotion in your body?

"Even though I feel this sadness in my heart, I Accept that I am feeling this way." (Tap on all the energy points)

Rate the intensity of your emotion on a scale of 0-10 (SUDS Rating-Subjective Units of Distress) 10 meaning – highest intensity (I feel terrible)   0 meaning – no intensity (I feel happy)

While rubbing the sore spot on your chest or tapping the side of either hand, repeat the following EFT Phrases aloud:

Even though I feel as if there is no way out for me and I don't know where to turn to, I deeply and completely/profoundly love, accept and forgive myself

Even though I feel so angry that I was left alone with a void, impossible to fill, I deeply and completely/profoundly love, accept and forgive myself anyway

Even though I feel as if this pain in my heart will never subside and I don't know how I am ever going to be able to move forward again, I deeply and completely/profoundly love, accept and forgive myself anyway

Now tap on the following energy points while repeating your negative reminder phrases: If possible tap on both sides of the face and body. (Use the palm of the hand to tap on the head and heart energy points)

Top of head and Heart: I feel this tremendous pain in my heart

Take 6 deep breaths. Say: "I'm ready to release all this pain from my heart, mind & body NOW!"

Top of eyebrow:	I was left all alone
Corner of eye:	I feel completely NUMB
Under eye:	My mind is paralyzed and I cannot have a clear thought
Under nose:	I'm very angry for being left alone
Under mouth:	I don't feel like doing anything
Collarbone:	I don't feel like living at all
Under arm:	This pain is so deep and overwhelming
Head & Heart:	I cannot keep going on like this

Take 6 deep breaths and say: "I choose to release all this pain from my heart, mind and body!"

Top of eyebrow:	I cry and cry all day long
Corner of eye:	I don't even want to get up in the morning
Under eye:	I don't want to get out of my home
Under nose:	I don't want to talk to anybody
Under mouth:	This pain in my heart is overwhelming me!
Collarbone:	I can't take it anymore
Under arm:	I'm so tired and burnt out
Head & Heart:	I'm scared about my future

Take 6 deep breaths. Say: "I acknowledge all those thoughts and emotions. I have a right to feel the way I feel. Now it's time to release all this pain from my heart, mind and body!"

How do you feel? Rate your emotional intensity level on a scale of 0-10, do several rounds until your intensity is down to zero.

Now it's time to reframe and expand your thinking and to open up possibilities:

Head & Heart:	What if I could relax just a little bit?
Top of eyebrow:	What if I could engage in new activities?
Corner of eye:	Maybe I can talk to somebody
Under eye:	Maybe there is somebody else who also understands my pain
Under nose:	What if I could ask for help, maybe it helps me to express what I am going through
Under mouth:	I am fully aware and acknowledge that it is going to take some time for me to feel better and to heal
Collarbone:	But maybe I can let go of some of this pain right NOW
Under arm:	What if I can begin to feel more energetic NOW
Head & Heart:	What if I started doing introducing a new ritual to my life… just being open to the possibility that I can let go of some of this pain

Take 6 deep breaths. Say: "I CAN release all this pain from my heart, mind and body!"

Top of eyebrow:	What if I could let go of some of this numbness and pain with every passing day
Corner of eye:	I am open to becoming free
Under eye:	I deserve to start having some joy in my heart
Under nose:	I deserve to embrace life again
Under mouth:	I have all the memories left and they will always be accessible in my heart
Collarbone:	I can think of all the good times we spent together at any given time. I'm beginning to allow a different form of connection between me and my love/friend/relative etc.
Under arm:	I am open to talk about the wonderful moments that we spent together
Head & Heart:	I am open to adopt a new sense of identity!

Take 6 deep breaths and say: "I wholeheartedly release all this pain from my heart, mind and body NOW!" Let everything go, you don't need to keep it anymore!

"Gratitude Process"

Start with the heart healing position and tap while repeating aloud:

I am grateful because I know that I can get better

I am grateful because I have wonderful friends that support me

I am grateful because I know that my heart is healing

I am grateful because I begin to sense some new beginnings that slowly will replaces my pain

I am grateful because I know that I will always love you and recall the happy memories

I am grateful because I know that I can give you a new place in my heart

QUICK GOOD MORNING GRATITUDE TAPPING

SOH: I deeply and completely love, accept and forgive myself!

I'm grateful for everything in my life that has led me to this moment as it has all been part of my unique destiny.

Eyes: I am grateful for who I am and acknowledge my emotions.
I am grateful for everything I experience in this lifetime, that helps me learn and grow
I am grateful for all life challenges, as they are opportunities for growth and a chance to evolve

Nose/mouth: I am grateful for my family & friends, their unconditional love & support
I am grateful for my blessed ancestors living on through my blood

Head/Heart: I am grateful for all my pets surrounding me and the gifts they give
I am grateful for the beauty of nature that indulges my senses every day

Under Arm: I am grateful for the possibility to choose thoughts that set me free

Head/Heart: I am grateful for the abundance I already have in my life and keep the door open for more
I am grateful for the ability to heal my body.

Under Arm: I am grateful for all the people who I have met for a moment or known deeply for they have all been my mirror and my teachers.

HHP.:   Thank you, thank you, thank you!

WHAT TO DO WHEN EFT DOESN'T WORK (GARY CRAIG)

When properly applied by an experienced practitioner, EFT (Meridian Tapping) has a very high success rate, usually over 90 percent. However, the initial success rate for newcomers usually starts around 50 percent. When EFT doesn't seem to be working, one or more of the following factors are usually involved:

- The Set-up was not performed completely enough (Psychological Reversal)
- You are trying to apply EFT to more than one thing at a time (jumping thoughts)
- The problem is being approached too generally/globally/not specific enough

The EFT Set-up Phrase was not performed completely enough The Set-up phrase together with tapping on the side of the hand corrects for Psychological Reversal (PR). When PR is present it blocks the whole process from working. So, if you aren't getting anywhere, try to tap the side of your hand harder and with more than just two fingers or rub the Sore Spot more vigorously while very *emphatically* saying the affirmation out loud.

A "secondary gain" (hidden benefit) / blocking belief is interfering A secondary gain is present when there is a "hidden benefit" or "hidden loss" to having or retaining the original issue. Examples of secondary gain include, "this issue keeps me safe," "I don't have to risk failure," "I get to avoid doing certain things by having this issue," and so on. Once you identify the secondary gain, you can tap on that directly. You should then be able to clear the original issue or problem more easily.

You are trying to apply EFT to more than one thing at a time It is very important to tune into only one problem at a time. You sometimes may accidentally try to apply EFT to more than one thing at a time without realizing it. This can happen when you are distracted and are thinking about something else while you are tapping on your problem. This can also happen when a second issue gets activated while attempting to address an original issue, even if you are not overtly aware of it.

Original memories need to be addressed first Sometimes, when we try to apply EFT to feelings about a current upset, it works fine. When this is not the case, it usually means that today's "charge" is really due to earlier similar formative experiences in our past. In that case, EFT usually works better and faster by applying it to those earlier experiences first. Then the current experience will either already have been cleared up or be amenable to clearing with tapping. You can look for early memories by asking yourself what the current situation reminds you of from your past.

When nothing works and you are totally overwhelmed, please get help!!!

See contact information in the front of the book.

SOME ENCOURAGING QUOTES

"Healing takes time, and asking for help is a courageous step." ~Mariska Hargitay

"Ask for help, not because you're weak, but because you want to remain strong." ~Les Brown

"Don't be afraid to ask questions. Don't be afraid to ask for help when you need it. I do that every day. Asking for help isn't a sign of weakness, it's a sign of strength. It shows you have the courage to admit when you don't know something, and then allows you to learn something new." ~Barack Obama (Education, Learning, School)

"Asking for help does not mean that we are weak or incompetent. It usually indicates an advanced level of honesty and intelligence." ~Anne Wilson Schaef, author.

"A little boy was having difficulty lifting a heavy stone.

His father came along just then.

Noting the boy's failure, he asked, "Are you using all your strength?"

"Yes, I am," the little boy said impatiently.

"No, you are not," the father answered.

"I am right here just waiting, and you haven't asked me to help you." ~Anon

REFERENCES

- Gary Craig www.emofree.com
- Roger Callahan www.tfttapping.com/ and http://rogercallahan.com
- Expressive Art Therapy www.goodtherapy.org/learn-about-therapy/
- Dance Therapy www.adta.org/
- Freestyle Dancing www.dancedivine.ca
- Non-dominant hand drawing www.umamara.blogspot.ca/2015/09/controlled-remote-viewing-farsight.html
- Ideograms www.federaljack.com/ebooks/Spirituality/ RV_Manual.pdf
- Pain Management www.selfhypnosis.com/using-nlp-to-reduce-pain/
- Surrogate Tapping www.emofree.com/eft-tutorial/tapping-bonus/surrogate
- Proxy Tapping - Dr. Mercola www.healthypets.mercola.com/sites/healthypets/
- Sway Test www.tapintoheaven.com/2stuff/stufstest.shtml
- Self Muscle Testing www.amybscher.com/self-muscle-testing-the-sway-test-or-idiometer-response/
- Emotions as Objects www.abh-abnlp.com/trance/scripts51.html
- Andrew Bryantwww.selfleadership.com/metaphors-stories-and-nlp/
- Use of Metaphors in Counseling www.narrativeinstitute.org
- Metaphor Therapy www.goodtherapy.org/learn-about-therapy/
- Dr. C. Malchiodi "Think Metaphor" www.psychologytoday.com/blog/arts-and-health
- Nick Ortner www.thetappingsolution.com
- Iyanla Vanzant – Forgiveness EFT www.hhemarketing.com/author/vanzant/web/
- Dr. Bruce Lipton www.brucelipton.com
- Gwenn Bonnell www.tapintoheaven.com
- Dance/Movement Therapy www.goodtherapy.org/learn-about-therapy/
- History of Tapping https://goe.ac/history_of_tapping.htm
- Susan Shanley www.energymed.org/hbank/handouts/meridian_tracing_affirmations.htm
- Dr. Bridgett Ross www.rosspsychology.com/blog/cognitive-therapy-101-core-beliefs

SHORT BIO

Monika Marguerite Lux is the originator of the BalanCHIng® Method which she developed over many years.

She is best known for her innate ability to intuitively identify the root cause of patterns keeping individuals stuck. Over the past decade, countless individuals have experienced deeply transformative and long-term shifts from her integrative formula of intuitive counseling combined with expressive art therapy and meridian tapping.

Monika's great passion is bringing healing to people who are dealing with trauma, grief and anxiety. She helps teenagers, adolescents, adults and families to find healthy perceptions of themselves and strengthen their relationships so they can know themselves as peaceful, complete, whole and safe.

Monika knows that no single approach is the right one for every individual, and so she has been trained in a range of modalities including Expressive Art Therapy, Systemic (Family) Constellations, Gestalt Therapy, Applied Kinesiology, Neuro Linguistic Programing and Emotional Freedom Technique.

Her educational background includes a German MA in Applied Psychology, a diploma as a Relaxation Therapist focused on Qigong and numerous energy medicine techniques like Usui Reiki (Master/Instructor Level), Matrix Energetics, Reconnection and many more.

In addition to her private practice, Monika is a blogger, speaker and workshop facilitator.

As a professional photographer, her most favorite non-traditional way of practicing meditation is to embark on a photo-taking spree with her best friend, the Cocker Spaniel "LUIGI" at the breath-taking natural locations on Vancouver Island where she resides right now.

Printed in the United States
By Bookmasters